SIGN
OF THE
KINGDOM

D0877514

SIGN
OF THE
KINGDOM

by Lesslie Newbigin

GRAND RAPIDS
WILLIAM B. EERDMANS PUBLISHING COMPANY

First published in Great Britain in 1980
under the title *Your Kingdom Come*
by John Paul The Preacher's Press

This American edition published 1981
through special arrangement with
John Paul The Preacher's Press
by Wm. B. Eerdmans Publishing Co.,
255 Jefferson Ave. S.E., Grand Rapids, MI 49503

Library of Congress Cataloging in Publication Data

Newbigin, James Edward Lesslie, Bp.
Sign of the kingdom.

Originally presented as the Waldström Lectures at the
Theological Seminary of the Swedish Covenant Church
at Lidingo in September 1979.
1. Kingdom of God — Addresses, essays, lectures.
I. Title.
BT94.N45   1981   231.7'2   80-28254
ISBN 0-8028-1878-1

Contents

Foreword

The Kingdom of God was the central theme of the preaching of Jesus as we find it in the New Testament. It has been, from time to time, a powerful theme in Christian thinking. Very specially it has been a dominant theme during one of the most dynamic periods of American history.

And yet it cannot be said that it has been the central theme in the great classical traditions of Christendom. It is not mentioned in the Apostles' Creed. The Nicene Creed says of Christ that 'his kingdom shall have no end', but does not use the phrase 'Kingdom of God'. The main traditions stemming from the Reformation have spoken of 'preaching the Gospel', or 'preaching Christ', but seldom of 'preaching the Kingdom'.

Liberal Protestants often reproached the Apostle Paul for having substituted the preaching of Christ for the preaching of the Kingdom, and something similar is happening today when we are told — as we often are — that we should concentrate on 'kingdom themes' rather than on 'church themes'. The message of the Kingdom has often been seen as something wider, more inclusive, less sectarian than the message of salvation through Jesus Christ.

The recent conference of the World Council of Churches in Australia, on the theme 'Your Kingdom Come', has brought the theme back again into the center of missionary thinking. The following pages were originally written in preparation for that meeting and were given at the Theological Seminary of the Swedish Covenant Church in Stockholm. I am grateful to the authorities of that seminary for permission to reproduce this material in English, for — although the Melbourne Conference is now past — the theme is still a very living one. Perhaps it will be enough to suggest three points at which this theme meshes immediately with burning contemporary concerns.

1. It is a commonplace that contemporary Christianity is subject to severe tensions between those on the one hand who see their faith as essentially concerned with the life of the spirit and regard the 'politicization of Christianity' as a grave deviation from the truth, and those on the other hand who regard a purely private and 'spiritual' religion as a betrayal of the biblical revelation. The proclamation of the kingdom, or reign of God, is obviously something which concerns the whole of life, and not only its religious dimension. Can the study of this biblical theme illuminate this contemporary struggle?

2. We live at a time when there is a strong insistence on 'people's participation', on 'power to the people', on the right of everyone to be consulted when decisions are made which affect him; and when there is, on the

other hand, a conservative swing in the direction of more authoritarian styles of leadership. The very word 'kingdom' calls up images of strong leadership 'from the top'. Can the study of kingship in the Bible help us to find the right kinds of leadership for our time?

3. One of the most important things happening in the world today is the world-wide renaissance of Islam. In many of its manifestations this is a passionate return to the conviction that God alone is to be honoured and obeyed, as against the 'permissive' styles of contemporary western culture. The very word 'Islam' means 'submission'. Islam is going to confront Christendom with some of its most burning questions during the next few decades. Can we learn to meet Islam with more understanding if we reflect afresh on what the kingship of God means in our own Scriptures?

Not only because the passionate discussions centering in the Melbourne Conference must and will continue in the churches, but also because these issues are of burning relevance to any Christian in our time, I hope that these slender studies of the theme may be of some continuing usefulness.

Selly Oak, Birmingham

LESSLIE NEWBIGIN

October 1980 *Bishop*

I

The Theme in Historical Perspective

The series of world missionary conferences, of which the Melbourne meeting is to be the next, provides a convenient way of charting the movements of thought in the Church about its world mission. If, using this index, one surveys the course of missionary thinking during the first eight decades of this century, it will be clear, I think, that the choice of the 'Kingdom' theme for the Melbourne meeting is a very timely one. I shall begin these reflections with a look at this history.

1. It is customary to date the rise of the modern ecumenical movement from the World Missionary Conference of Edinburgh 1910. It is instructive, however, to remember that this meeting was initially scheduled to be the 'Third Ecumenical Missionary Conference', following as it did upon the meetings in London (1890) and New York (1900). The word "ecumenical" was dropped from the title in deference to the wishes of the Anglo-Catholic elements in the Church of England who felt that this adjective could only be applied to a truly ecumenical council, and so the meeting was simply re-titled 'World Missionary Conference'.

If we look at the missionary literature of the period

of these three world meetings, and even at the documents of Edinburgh itself, it is clear that the overwhelming emphasis is upon the duty and privilege of all Christians to bring the Gospel to every human being with the intention and hope of bringing every one to personal conversion to Jesus as Lord and Saviour. There was, undoubtedly, a great deal of discussion about the exact meaning of the famous "Watchword" which played such a decisive role in the rise of the Student Volunteer Missionary movement up to the time of Edinburgh. 'The Evangelisation of the World in this Generation' did not mean the *conversion* of the whole world; conversion can only be the work of God the Holy Spirit. What it did mean was the bringing to every person, so far as possible, of the good news of Jesus Christ. This — it was held — was now possible in view of the new means of communication available throughout every part of the globe. If it was possible, it was mandatory. Each generation of humankind must hear the message in its time from those of the same generation who have been entrusted with it. If these latter fail to discharge this trust for their own generation, they have been unfaithful.

It was a noble passion, which sent thousands of men and women to all parts of the world, and which had as its fruit what William Temple called 'the great new fact of our time'. These often misinterpreted words of Temple did not refer to the ecumenical *movement*; they referred to the fact that the Christian Church had become for the first time a truly world-wide community. That fact was the necessary pre-condition for the birth and growth of a truly ecumenical movement. Without this great missionary outpouring the very preconditions for an ecumenical movement would not have existed. That ought not to be forgotten.

2. There is much to reflect upon in this period, but I hurry on to the second of the series which began at Edinburgh — the World Missionary Conference of Jerusalem 1928. The scene has changed almost out of recognition. The confidence of the 'Christian West' has been shattered beyond repair. The world religions are no longer seen as the adversaries from whose grip men and women must be rescued by the Gospel. Rather the great adversary is seen to be that secularism which has become the West's most influential export. It is *not* true, as sometimes stated, that Jerusalem advocated an alliance of the world's religions to combat secularism — although there were powerful voices which spoke in those terms. In its positive statement of the missionary task Jerusalem placed its main emphasis upon the life of nations as a whole, rather than upon the destiny of individual souls. This is the most striking contrast with the language of Edinburgh. The following extract from the 'Message' of the Conference (written by William Temple) will indicate its central thrust.

> Jesus himself said, 'I am come that they might have life, and that they might have it more abundantly', and our experience corroborates it. He has become life to us. We would share that life.

> We are assured that Christ comes with an offer of life to men and to nations. We believe that in him the shackles of moral evil and guilt are broken from human personality and that men are made free, and that such personal freedom lies at the basis of the

freeing of society from cramping customs and blighting social practices and political bondages, so that in Christ men and societies and nations may stand up free and complete.

We find in Christ, and especially in his cross and resurrection, an inexhaustible source of power hat makes us hope when there is no hope. We believe that through it men and societies and nations that have lost their moral nerve to live will be quickened into life.

We have a pattern in our minds as to what form that life should take. We believe in a Christ-like world. We know nothing better, we can be content with nothing less. We do not go to the nations called non-Christian because they are the worst of the world and they alone are in need — we go because they are a part of the world and share the same human need — the need for redemption from ourselves and from sin, the need to have life complete and abundant and to be re-made after this pattern of Christlikeness. We desire a world in which Christ will not be crucified but where his Spirit shall reign.

During the years following the Jerusalem Conference no text was more often quoted in missionary addresses than the one quoted here — 'I am come that they might have life and have it more abundantly'. And 'abundant life' was interpreted to refer to the whole human situation — economic, cultural, political and technological as well as personal and spiritual. It enabled John R. Mott to include in his beloved phrase 'the larger evangelism' almost everything that a later age was to call 'development'. I well remember a missionary colleague in the mid 1930s complaining to me that whenever he took up an article on evangelism to read, he found that by the time he had reached the middle of the second page he was reading about a new way of breeding pigs or poultry. That was characteristic of the missiology of the time — at least in the Anglo-Saxon world of which I was a native.

3. But meanwhile quite other forces were arising. Already at the time of the Jerusalem meeting a separate meeting of the Continental European delegates had met at Cairo and had protested against the one-sided character of the preliminary Conference documents. Their protest represented the powerful new theological currents which were flowing strongly especially in the German-speaking world under the leadership of Karl Barth. They called for a recognition of the radical difference between the message of the Gospel and any programme of merely earthly betterment. Their most effective spokesman at Jerusalem was the Dutch missionary H. Kraemer who put a number of very sharp questions to the underlying assumptions of the majority at the meeting, and who was to have the opportunity ten years later to make his case in a way that compelled world-wide attention.

But meanwhile on the other side of the Atlantic the movements against which the Continentals were issuing their warnings continued with growing strength. With the support of John R. Mott, and under the theological leadership of Rufus M. Jones and William E. Hocking, the 'Laymen's Enquiry into Foreign Missions' was launched. This enlisted the support of prominent American business men and undertook a very far-reaching investigation into the work of (chiefly North

American) foreign missions all over the world. Their
report 'Re-thinking Missions', published in 1932 represented such an extreme development of one line of
missiology that it brought the debate right into the
heart of the Anglo-Saxon world and evoked the im-
mediate protest of such trusted American missionary
leaders as John A. Mackay. 'Re-thinking Missions' sees
the significance of the missionary enterprise in terms
of its contribution to 'social progress' and 'the communication of spiritual values'. The Report deprecates
evangelism as traditionally understood and advocated
rather the sharing of spiritual resources among the
spiritually minded of all religions. It recognises that
there are problems in the world but is confident that
'while these problems are being worked out, the spirit
of their solution is present'. 'Through Jesus and through
such wills as his, God works through human history
bringing men towards unity in a love which is universal in its sweep.'

The central message of the Report may be indicated
by quoting the closing sentences of its section on 'The
Aim of Missions'.

> The message presents a way of life and thinking
> which the Christian conceives, not as his way alone,
> but as a way for all men. It is a way which may
> enter without violence the texture of their living and
> transform it from within. As Christianity shares this
> faith with men of all faiths, they become changed
> into the same substance. The names which now sep-
> arate them lose their divisive meaning; and there
> need be no loss of the historic thread of devotion
> which unites each to its own origins and inspirations.

> The goal to which this way leads may be variously

described, most perfectly perhaps in the single phrase, Thy Kingdom come. This is and has always been the true aim of Christian missions.

Its detail varies as we learn more of what is involved in it. It means to us now, as always, saving life. It means representing to the Orient the spiritual sources of Western civilisation, while its other aspects, technical and material, are being represented so vigorously in other ways. It means paving the way for international friendship through a deeper understanding. It means trying more definitely to strengthen our own hold on the meaning of religion in human life. Should we try to express this conception in a more literal statement it might be this:

> To seek with people of other lands a true knowledge of God, expressing in life and word what we have learned through Jesus Christ, and endeavouring to give effect to his spirit in the life of the world.

It will be noted from the above extract that 'Thy Kingdom come!' is accepted as the key phrase which defines the aim of missions. But, in this interpretation, the Kingdom is seen as something very much broader than can be defined by allegiance to the Person of Jesus Christ. Jesus is seen as illustrative of a 'spirit' which is everywhere at work in the world, and the work of missions is to join with and 'endeavour to give effect to' the work of this spirit. As this worked out in practice it meant that preaching, evangelism, conversion, baptism and the building up of the Church became relatively peripheral concerns. The centre of the picture was full of activities designed to promote mutual understanding and to furnish the less advanced na-

tions with the amenities which western technology
made available.

The weaknesses of this approach were obvious. If
I may speak personally, I can vividly remember the
growing sense of nausea with which I became overwhelmed in the flood-tide of this kind of liberalism,
and the sense of relief which came when I began to
hear different notes sounded — the message of the Gospel as a message of radical judgment and mercy, of
liberation from the power of sin, of a joy already given,
of the Church as a totally committed fellowship which
could say 'I believe . . .' in the midst of all the overwhelming powers of the rising paganism of Europe.
And in this I was of course reflecting an experience
that was most strongly felt in those parts of Europe
most directly exposed to the new totalitarian ideologies — especially those of the right. In this new situation much that had been taken for granted was suddenly
brought to the centre of attention. It became clear that
the Church was no longer the religious aspect of western society. It was a besieged citadel, surrounded by
aggressive enemies. Neither individual piety nor a social gospel was enough to enable people to face the
organised communal power of the new paganism. The
Confessing Church in Germany provided a paradigm
of the kind of response that was called for. There was
no place now for a kind of Christianity that thought
it could get along without the Church. So, when the
Oxford Conference on Church Community and State
met in 1937, the watchword that came forth from its
deliberations was nothing that looked continuous with
the earlier discussions. 'Let the Church be the Church'.
That phrase — startlingly simple — was to set the tone

of ecumenical thinking for the next 25 years. The Church — so long taken for granted or ignored in missionary discussion — was seen as the bastion of truth in a swirling sea of falsehood, the City of God among the furies of the false gods.

4. This new mood was immediately apparent in the meetings of the third in the series of world missionary conferences — Tambaram 1938. In contrast to the language of both Edinburgh and Jerusalem, we find here a new way of speaking about mission. At every point the Conference speaks of the mission of the Church. 'The Church is called to live and to give life in a world shaken to its foundations. . . .' 'The Church must conduct its mission. . . .' 'It is God's will to utter his words and to accomplish his deeds through the Church.' 'We are constrained to declare to a baffled and needy world that the Christian Church, under God, is its greatest hope.' These are typical extracts from the 'Message' of the Conference. The Church is the subject of almost every significant sentence about mission. And this was to provide the model for missionary discussion during the next two decades. Almost every issue was discussed in terms of the dichotomy of Church and World. The most powerful theological voice was that of Karl Barth, who had significantly changed the title of his *magnum opus* from 'Christian Dogmatics' to 'Church Dogmatics'. There were, of course, protests. At the time of the Tambaram Conference the veteran Indian missionary E. Stanley Jones carried on a vigorous argument that missions were taking a wrong road, that their proper concern was not the Church but the Kingdom of God. But this represented a view which was

felt to be out of date. At least in those circles most
strongly influenced by events in Europe there was no
desire to follow any further the road trodden by the
'Laymen's Enquiry', and the theme of the Kingdom
seemed to have already been pre-empted by those who
went that way. So Tambaram signalled the beginning
of the long period of Church-centered missiology.

To this period belong a whole series of very far-
reaching changes in the structure of missions. The
phrase 'Younger Churches' appeared with more and
more frequency. The attempt was made to see everything from their point of view. Through various slow
and sometimes agonising metamorphoses missions de-
volved their responsibilities upon the churches which
had grown up through their work. National missionary
councils became councils of churches. In the sending
countries of the West missions (hitherto very much the
enthusiasm of a minority in the churches) were in-
creasingly recognised as the responsibility of the Church
itself. The International Missionary Council became a
part of the World Council of Churches. The theme of
church unity became a living one in missionary circles.
The question of the relation between missions and 'in-
ter-church aid' became a burning one. As the latter
concept moved into the centre of missionary thinking,
some sending agencies changed the name of their
workers from 'missionary' to 'fraternal worker'.

5. The first major public challenge to this church-centric missiology came at the World Missionary Conference of Willingen in 1952. This meeting had been
called — significantly — to discuss 'The Missionary Obligation of the Church'. In the Group which was spe-

cially charged with developing this theme a powerful attack upon the dominant missiology was led by Hans Hoekendijk of the Netherlands and Paul Lehmann of the United States. Hoekendijk's missiology centred on the concept of *shalom* as God's gift to the world. Rather than speak of the mission of the Church one should speak of the mission of God and see the Church as a by-product of this primal mission. The mission of God is much greater than the Church and is not limited to the Church. Some sentences from the report which the Group presented to the Conference will indicate the lines along which it was working.

> We are convinced that it is not only possible but also necessary to discern by faith the ways in which God is exercising his sovereignty in our time: in *personal life,* where he takes hold of deeds performed faithfully amidst tragedy and frustration and weaves them into his on-going purpose; in *the movements of political and social life,* where he both shows his judgment and also confronts whole societies with new opportunities of living; in *the processes of scientific discovery,* where he opens up new ranges of creation, with their promises of hope and possibilities of disaster.
>
> In such and other ways of his action, God is carrying out his judgment and redemption in the revolutionary movements of our time.

Language of this kind was to become very familiar a dozen years later, but at that time it had not been articulated in a way which could be accepted. The Group was trying to express a concept of mission which was much wider than the accepted church-centric one, but the Conference was not ready to accept it. The report was received but not adopted, and in its place a substitute document was accepted which was more in line with the contemporary thinking. It spoke of the source of mission in the being of the Triune God, and contained the phrase — often to be quoted in later years — 'There is no participation in Christ without participation in his mission to the world. . . .' This expressed a total commitment of the Church to mission, but did not answer the question whether, and in what way, the mission is greater than the Church. That question continued to occupy the minds of those who were not satisfied with the prevalent view.

6. The point at which a confident and affirmative answer to that question was publicly made was, perhaps, the Strasbourg Conference of 1960 on 'The Life and Mission of the Church'. This had been organised by the World's Student Christian Federation, whose leaders (notably D. T. Niles and Philippe Maury) believed that there was an important ecumenical consensus about the missionary nature of the Church, and that this had to be communicated in an effective way to the coming generation of students. The official title of the Conference was completely in line with the missiology which had dominated the scene since Tambaram 1938. But the event was to prove quite other than the expectations. The younger generation of student leaders were far more eager to follow the line which had been adumbrated at Willingen by Hoekendijk. His address to the Conference provided some of its most characteristic notes. The time had come, he said 'to move out of the traditional church structures in open, flexible and mobile groups' and 'to begin radically to de-

sacralise the Church'. Strasbourg sounded the characteristic notes of the ensuing decade by insisting that the secular is the primary field of God's redemptive activity, and that it is by involvement in what God is doing in the secular world, rather than in seeking to draw men into the Church, that we can participate in God's mission.

This exaltation of the secular was to become one of the most characteristic notes in missionary thinking during the 1960s. Arendt van Leeuwen's book 'Christianity in World History' (1964) interpreted world history in terms of the impact of the biblical message upon the 'ontocratic' societies in which men live before they meet the Lord of history, and concluded with the claim that the contemporary movement of secularisation was the present form of this impact. 'The technological revolution is the evident and inescapable form in which the whole world is now confronted with the most recent phase of Christian history. In and through this form Christian history becomes world history.' A year later Harvey Cox celebrated 'The Secular City' as the sphere of God's liberating activity. And the study of 'The Missionary Structure of the Congregation' which had been taken up in the context of the church-centric missiology of the previous decade, became — as it developed in the 1960s — a further adumbration of the theme of secularity. It insisted that the traditional view (expressed so sharply at Tambaram) that God does his work of blessing for the world through the Church has to be abandoned; rather God addresses the Church through the world. It is the world which writes the agenda for the Church, and the order is not God-Church-World, but rather God-World-Church. One might indeed have been pardoned for getting the impression that God was to be found, and to be heard speaking, everywhere in the world except in the Church!

And by the end of the decade there was wide agreement about what God was saying to the Church. By the listening Church (if it could be persuaded to listen) three sounds would be clearly heard: the cry of the victims of hunger and political oppression; the angry protest of the victims of racial discrimination; the growing symphony of renaissant world religions. The first two of these dominated the Fourth Assembly of the World Council of Churches at Uppsala (1968) and especially its Section on 'Renewal in Mission'.

7. The opening sentence of the Report of this Section is as follows. 'We belong to a humanity that cries passionately and articulately for a fully human life.' The Report goes on to define mission as participation in the struggle for such a fully human life in the name and in the power of the true Man — Jesus Christ. Consequently the old conception of 'mission fields', understood as areas where the Gospel had not yet been heard, is replaced by the conception of 'points for mission', understood as situations where the struggle for humanisation has to take place. These points may be inside of the Church or outside of it; the front-line in this battle runs right through the Church.

The WCC's Division of World Mission and Evangelisation was already in 1968 deeply involved — through its Urban Industrial Mission unit — in the struggles of many groups of oppressed and exploited people, especially in the cities. It was soon to take up Paulo Freire's programme of 'conscientisation' and to be fully involved in the 'liberation theology' which was being developed in Latin America and elsewhere. The WCC's 'Programme to Combat Racism' — also a product of the Uppsala Assembly — compelled all its members churches to face the question of their attitude to the struggle of oppressed people for full humanity. After 1500 years in which — at least in the western world — Christianity had always been seen as part of the established order and a major contributor to its stability, the churches were being challenged to take at many points an 'anti-establishment' stance. The Exodus story became more and more frequently the key to unlock the fundamental message of the Bible; it was a message of deliverance from the oppressor. The churches, which often seemed to belong rather to the court of Pharaoh than to the camp of Moses, were summoned to identify themselves unequivocally with the aspirations of the oppressed. The old cry 'Come ye out from among them and be separate' was heard again — but this time in the name not of evangelical purity but in the name of commitment to the cause of the oppressed. The real works of God (as outlined programmatically in the words of Jesus in the Nazareth synagogue) were to be found outside the churches rather than within them; the call was therefore to create new 'base communities' rooted in the life of the ordinary people and uncompromised by the long alliance between the Church and the Establishment.

8. Movements of thought are slow, and there are few sharp breaks. Nevertheless as the eighth decade of the century moves towards its close one can detect some changes in this climate of thought. There is much less

confidence in the validity of western science and technology than there was ten years ago. The books of
Harvey Cox and van Leeuwen seem now to belong to
a past age. The recent (MIT) conference on 'Science,
Faith and the Future' witnessed a very strong attack,
especially from representatives of the Third World,
upon the pretensions of western science and technology. In the western world there is a strong interest in
the dimension of the transcendant and a search — which
takes many and bizarre forms — for a new spirituality.
The 'death of God' is now felt to have been a characteristic non-event of the 1960s. The Bangkok Conference of the WCC took as its theme 'Salvation Today'
and — without muting any of the thunderous notes
sounded at Uppsala on the theme of justice — the Conference was concerned to ask about the reality of a
present experience of salvation in the midst of the
struggle for justice. And when the Fifth Assembly met
at Nairobi in 1975, the change in atmosphere from
Uppsala was striking. It was expressed by Philip Pot-
ter in the following way: 'At Uppsala the mood was
one of Exodus, going out to change the structures of
society. . . . Now we find ourselves in the wilderness.
. . . A pilgrim people in conflict and penury, we have
discovered a need for spirituality — a spirituality of
penitence and hope.'

9. 'Penitence and hope': that surely is the mood in
which the theme of the next world missionary conference has been chosen. 'Your kingdom come' — with this
prayer the ecumenical missionary community enters
the next decade. I hope that reflection on the course of
missionary thinking during the first eight decades of

the century will help us to see both the possibilities to
be pursued and also the dangers to be avoided in the
development of this theme as a guide to missionary
praxis in the decade ahead. Let me, as a conclusion to
this brief glance at history, and as an introduction to
what follows share with you the following three
reflections.

(a) I am sure that it is right to go back to the Kingdom of God as the central theme. The church-centric
thinking about missions has had a long run. I believe
that it has been fruitful. I think that it has lessons to
teach which (at least) western protestant missionary
thinking has still to absorb. I am sure, for example,
that the Orthodox have a great deal to teach the rest
of Christendom about the role of the Church in God's
mission which we have still to learn. But there are at
least two reasons for which I am glad that this theme
has been chosen. The first is simply that it was the
central theme of Jesus' preaching. It has therefore a
primacy which cannot be denied. The frequent misunderstanding and misapplication of this teaching, especially in the missiology of the Anglo-Saxon world in
the years between the wars, is not a reason for turning
away from it, but a reason for returning to the teaching
of Jesus with fresh and chastened attention. The second reason for welcoming the theme is that it points
to the universality of the Gospel and challenges the
timid privatisation of religion which has become so
general in western Christianity. The theme challenges
us to recognise the universal and 'holistic' character of
the gift and the claim of God in Jesus Christ.

(b) The brief survey which we have made of missionary thinking in the earlier decades of this century

will have highlighted, I hope, two dangers which must
be avoided in the development of the theme. The first
is the separation of the Kingdom from the Person of
Jesus. We have seen how the Laymen's Report regarded the message of the Kingdom as something tran-
scending the Person of Jesus and therefore to be
welcomed as delivering missions from the charge of
absolutising a particular name and tradition. During
the period which produced the Laymen's Report it was
explained *ad nauseam* that whereas Jesus had preached
the Kingdom, Paul had preached Christ — thereby sub-
stituting a different message for that which Jesus had
proclaimed. The truth is that if Paul and the early
Church had simply continued to preach the Kingdom
they would have misrepresented what Jesus was, did
and taught. It was not just that 'Kingdom of God' was
a Hebraic phrase which would be obscure to Gentile
hearers. It was a more fundamental matter even than
this. It was that 'the kingdom of God' was no longer —
as it had been before the coming of Jesus — an abstract
idea; it was no longer simply the fact that God reigns
(which might almost be a tautology). The kingdom
now had a name and a face, the name and the face of
Jesus. The question 'What does it mean to say "God
reigns"?', the question of the manner and form of the
reign of God, had now been answered — answered in
the Person of Jesus. To preach Jesus, therefore, was to
preach the Kingdom of God as it truly is. To have failed
to do so would have been to misrepresent the mission
and message of Jesus. And our brief survey has surely
given us enough illustrations of the fact that when the
message of the Kingdom is divorced from the Person
of Jesus, it becomes a programme or an ideology, but

not a gospel. In Pauline terms, the preaching of the Kingdom then becomes a preaching of the law.

The second danger to be avoided is the separation of the Kingdom from the Church. It is clear that they cannot and must not be confused, certainly not identified. But they must also not be separated. From the beginning the announcement of the Kingdom led to a summons to follow and so to the formation of a community. It is the community which has begun to taste (even only in foretaste) the reality of the Kingdom which can alone provide the hermeneutic of the message. In a recent article on the theme of the Kingdom, Raymond Fung of the Urban Industrial Mission team in Hong Kong has written: 'I believe the Kingdom of God suggests that Christian Mission should take the form of community, an environment in which God's rule is recognised, whereby the values of justice, peace and love operate.' Without the hermeneutic of such a living community, the message of the Kingdom can only become — once again — an ideology and a programme; it will not be a gospel.

(c) It is important that the Theme is in the form of a prayer — the most central of all Christian prayers. This is important for two reasons. In the first place, it centres everything in the living God himself — the living God in whom alone we trust, whose faithful and gracious action we wait for, expect and rely on. And, secondly, we are thereby protected from converting the message into an ideology, a programme, a law — in other words, from putting our trust in anything other than God.

With these preliminary reflections we now turn to look at the Theme in its biblical perspective.

II

The Theme in its Biblical Perspective

Kingship is not a particularly popular commodity in our world. The ancient world was full of kings and queens; we have few of them and — highly as we cherish them — we limit their powers rather strictly. The ancient idea of kingship as the exercise of sovereign rule over others by a single individual is not one for which our world has much room.

When we turn to the Old Testament it is clear that the attitude to kingship is profoundly ambiguous. It is clear — and it is natural — that the Hebrews were well aware of, and were influenced by the ideas of kingship developed in the surrounding nations — Assyria, Babylon, Persia — and, very specially, by the fantastic development of the institution of kingship in Egypt, that civilisation with which Israel was always in such an intimate relation either of love or of hate. In this tradition of kingship, the king is the one to whom total obedience is due, and from whom one can expect protection, help, and the righting of wrongs. Using H. H. Farmer's phrase, one could almost say that the king was the one who could make the absolute demand and who could offer the final succour. In this sense of kingship it is clear that Israel could acknowledge no king except Yahweh. This was fundamental to the faith of Israel.

Against this background, the institution of an earthly kingship is seen alternately as an appointment by Yahweh for the good of his people and as an act of apostasy from the true kingship of Yahweh to an illegitimate and fatal imitation of the pagan kings. On the one hand there is the heavy emphasis in the Book of Judges upon the chaos that overwhelmed Israel when they had no king to lead them ('In those days there was no king in Israel; every man did what was right in his own eyes' — Jg. 21:25, etc.) and upon the graciousness of Yahweh in raising up judges to rule over them and overcome this chaos. It is in line with this thinking that the elevation of Saul to the kingship is seen as a gracious action of Yahweh (I Sam. 9:15–17). On the other hand there is the long diatribe of I Samuel 8 in which the popular demand for a king is seen as an act of apostasy from Israel's true King — Yahweh alone.

There is much that is obscure here, and I am no Old Testament scholar, but it seems clear that both these traditions have to be taken seriously in seeking to understand the idea of the kingdom of God, and also that after the tragedy of Saul, Israel's faith in Yahweh as the one who is always faithful to his promise was very early linked to the kingship of David and his house. The promise that Yahweh would establish and maintain a true kingship in and for Israel through the house of David is a very important part of Israel's faith from a very early time. Thus one must say that in the figure of David the idea of earthly kingship has a very important place in the whole of Old Testament faith.

In later Judaism two distinct strands of thought about the kingship of Yahweh are to be discerned. On the one hand (a) Yahweh is in fact now and always king over all, but it is possible to be ignorant of his kingship, or to fail to recognise it, or — alternatively — to accept for oneself the yoke of Yahweh's sovereignty *(malkuth)* and live under it. In the end, however, the kingship of Yahweh will be manifest to all and there will no longer be any possibility of avoiding or ignoring it. This kind of thinking leads into the apocalyptic vision of the End. On the other hand (b) there is a strand of thought which continues the theme of the Davidic kingship. This looks to a future in which a Son of David will rule over Israel, and even over the nations, bringing in a wonderful age of prosperity, justice and peace. There are very many sketches of such an age in the prophetic books and in the Psalms.

It is, I think, important to draw attention to the second of these two strands in the Old Testament, because it has been so completely overlooked in recent missiology, which has tried to relate everything to the Exodus theme in which the king (Pharaoh) is the embodiment of all that is evil. When this line is pursued in isolation, rule of any kind is defined as 'structural violence', and the exercise of coercive authority such as all political rule requires, is equated simply with oppression. As against this it is surely important to pay attention to what the Old Testament has to say about true kingship. When this is totally ignored and the church identifies itself entirely with resistance to authority, the result will surely be that described in

the Book of Judges. And in fact the Exodus story itself
is misunderstood if it is read as the story of the revolt
of the oppressed against their ruler. There is little sign
in the story that the Israelites had been adequately
conscientised! The story is in fact the story of a true
king (Yahweh) exercising his power over an evil king,
and bringing Israel under allegiance to his own true
kingship. The story of the Exodus is sealed in the giving and accepting of the Law.

In both these strands of interpretation it is important to note that the key word *malkuth* refers primarily
to the *fact* of rule, and only secondarily to the sphere
of that rule. Those who were familiar with India before
1947 will recognise the same usage in the word so
often used then — 'the Raj'. This did not mean primarily 'India'; it meant the fact of British rule over India.
In this respect the Greek word *Basileia* correctly trans-
lates the original; the primary reference is to the *fact*
of God's sovereign rule.

What, then, against this background, did it mean
that Jesus began his public ministry with the words
'The time is fulfilled, and the kingdom *(malkuth, basileia)* of God is at hand; repent and believe in the
gospel'?

Five points, I believe, are to be noted.

1. This is the announcement of a happening. It is news.
It is not the launching of a programme for which sup-
porters are needed. It is not the propounding of an
ideology or a philosophy or a religious doctrine. It is
in the strictest sense an announcement of an event, of
a happening.

2. The subject of this happening is the *malkuth*

Yahweh, the kingship of the God of Israel. On this two things are to be said.

(a) The news is public news. It concerns the 'public sector'. It does not refer to the sphere of religion. The rule of Yahweh is not limited to the 'private sector'. It is not limited to the religious life of people. It is cosmic in its scope. It embraces everything in the world of nature and of history. We are not, therefore, looking at the development of one strand in the bundle of human affairs; we are looking at something which concerns the totality of human and cosmic history.

(b) The fact that Yahweh is King is not, in itself, news. It is part of the fundamental faith of Israel, celebrated in psalm and liturgy. What, then, is new? The news is that this sovereignty has now become present reality with which one has to come to terms. It is no longer something remote, something belonging to the end of time, or to a transmundane sphere of reality. It has become present reality. In what sense is this so? The unfolding of the following story is the answer to that question.

3. The announcement is linked to a call to 'repent' — to execute a U-turn of the whole mind, to face in the opposite direction. The call to repent has been almost trivialised in conventional evangelical piety, as though it meant simply a call to give up a few bad habits. What is involved here is something very much more drastic. The whole nation is facing the wrong way. It is looking for salvation in the wrong direction. It has its heart on the wrong things. As long as this is so, the reign of God must be hidden from its view. Only when there has been a complete turn-round, so that the na-

tion is facing in the opposite direction, is there the possibility of responding to the message.

4. But the response will be — not open vision — but faith. Those who make this U-turn will be enabled to *believe* the good news — the news that the reign of God is now a present reality. We shall learn as we go through the story that this faith itself is a gift to those who are called to be the witnesses of the presence of the reign of God in Jesus. It is not simply to be understood as a human decision among various human possibilities; it is a gift of God to those who are *called*.

5. This calling begins immediately. In the immediately following verses of Mark (1:16ff) we see Jesus calling by name those whom he has chosen — Peter and Andrew, James and John. In other words, the announcement of the presence of the reign of God does not remain a disembodied verbal message. Nor is it left simply to the inclination of any individuals who happen to be interested. There is a personal calling by name addressed to those whom Jesus wills: 'Peter, follow me.' As the story unfolds we find that a clear distinction is made between those who merely follow because they are interested, and those whom Jesus has chosen and called. The distinction is expressed with precision in the words attributed to Jesus by the Fourth Evangelist: 'You did not choose me: I chose you and appointed you that you should go and bear fruit' (John 15:16). The calling and choosing is not for themselves; it is that they may bear fruit, or — in the language of the Synoptic Gospels — that they may become fishers of men.

Such is 'the beginning of the Gospel' according to Mark. Jesus sets out on his ministry. Around him is the small group of those whom he has chosen and called, and beyond this is the larger crowd of those who follow with more or less understanding and enthusiasm.

The understanding and enthusiasm are under severe strain. Things do not turn out as expected. The Kingdom of God is not obviously present. There is a persistent demand for explanation. 'Why does he keep us in the dark? Why does he not make it plain? What *is* this "reign of God"? Where is it to be found? Can he not make it plain?'

Yes — and no! There are the parables: 'The Kingdom of God is like . . .' But these leave the majority still guessing. When Jesus is asked why he uses parables instead of giving plain explanations, he replies with the terrible words of Isaiah 6 which promise that the word of God will *not* be understood (Mark 4:10–12). The secret of the Kingdom is 'given' to those who have been chosen and called; to the rest it is riddles. As compared with the version in Matthew, Mark puts the saying in its sharpest possible form ('*so that* they may indeed see but not perceive . . .'), and as Mark's text reflects the Aramaic form it is more likely to be authentic.

Not only are there the parables, there are also the 'mighty works'. But these too are ambiguous. When John the Baptist sends messengers to ask 'Are you he who is to come, or shall we look for another?' (Luke 7:18ff), Jesus answers with a catena of quotations from Isaiah 35 — the blind see, the lame walk, the deaf hear; the signs of the kingdom are there to see — but then adds 'And blessed is he who takes no offence at me'. These signs do not *demonstrate* the presence of the Kingdom; they can also be occasions for stumbling, for scandal. They can be interpreted as works of the devil.

Neither the parables nor the 'mighty works' are un-ambiguous evidence of the presence of the Kingdom. It is to those who are chosen and called, those to whom it is 'given', those who are 'blessed', that parables and mighty works become pointers to the mystery of the Kingdom. For this presence of the Kingdom is both an unveiling and a veiling. Jesus, in the contingency and particularity of his human being, is the presence of the Kingdom; but that very presence can be a riddle or a scandal.

I have been following Mark's account of the beginning of the ministry. Having now looked at a passage from Luke, let us turn to his — somewhat different — account of the beginning. We turn to the famous declaration in the synagogue of Nazareth, often spoken of as the 'Nazareth Manifesto'.

> Jesus opened the book and found the place where it was written 'The Spirit of the Lord is upon me, because he has anointed me to preach good news to the poor. He has sent me to proclaim release to the captives and recovering of sight to the blind, to set at liberty those who are oppressed, to proclaim the acceptable year of the Lord.'

This famous passage is very frequently quoted in comtemporary writing as the basis for an interpretation of the ministry of Jesus as the launching of a 'people's movement' for liberation, a movement which inevitably led on to a confrontation with the 'Establishment'. (See, for example, International Review of Mission, No. 270, pp. 110ff.) These words of Jesus, which he takes from the prophet Isaiah and makes his own, are seen as the manifesto for a popular movement of revolutionary change in the established economic and political order.

I suggest that this is a too simplistic transference of contemporary ideas to the text. A reading of the whole story, including the sequel, will give, I think, a somewhat different picture. The manifesto, if we give it that name, is the proclamation of a true king in the messianic tradition. It is the function of a just ruler, a true king, to bring deliverance to the oppressed. This is an application of the Davidic strand in Old Testament teaching about the Kingdom. And the reasons for which Jesus' words were rejected is not (as far as this pericope is concerned) because he was on the side of the poor against the rich. The reasons are twofold. In the first place, he offended against nationalist sentiment (verses 23–27). The suggestion that God's first care might not be Israel but the Gentiles was the first thing that aroused the popular fury against him. In the second place they took offence at his person. 'Is not this Joseph's son?' they said. And so the rejection at Nazareth was not an action of 'the Establishment'; the story seems to make it quite clear that it was a 'people's movement' that tried to destroy him at the very outset.

There is no doubt whatever that the Gospels carry forward the Old Testament faith that 'God has a bias in favour of the poor'. This comes out clearly at many points in the story. But there is an important difference between two possible ways of viewing this. Contemporary exegesis tends to see it in the framework of the Marxist class analysis which divides all humanity into two sharply defined classes — oppressors and oppressed. From this point of view Jesus is seen as launching a movement of the oppressed, a 'people's movement' which naturally arouses the hostility of the established powers. And there are indeed evidences of a 'people's movement' beginning to take shape around Jesus. What is striking is that Jesus emphatically distances himself from this. The account in the Fourth Gospel of the events following the feeding of the 5,000 makes this very clear. He refuses to be part of a messianic movement in this sense. Rather the story has to be interpreted in the framework of the basic Old Testament conviction that Yahweh is the true king who intervenes to establish the cause of the oppressed against their oppressors. The source of disturbance is this kingly intervention from above, not a popular movement from below. And the cause of stumbling is that this intervention is embodied in the person of this man Jesus, who does not conform to the popular expectations of the Messiah. The long argument of John 6 culminates in the almost total abandonment of Jesus by his followers because Jesus insists that the true manna, the true bread with which the Father feeds the hungry, is himself, 'my flesh'. The cause of stumbling is the Person of Jesus himself.

To insist upon this is not to pass any judgment on the necessity for Christian action for justice in economic and political affairs; it is simply to ask that the Gospel story be interpreted by means of its actual background and presuppositions. The Marxist class analysis does not provide this. Indeed one could properly go on to point out that the people to whom the kingdom is promised — the halt and the lame, the blind and deaf, the lepers and the outcastes — are *not* by any means the proletariat in Marxist terms. They are not the possible bearers of revolutionary justice. They are more akin to Marx's *lumpenproletariat,* from whom no revolution comes.

Jesus does overturn accepted standards. He does put down the mighty from their seats, and raise up the humble and meek. But that overturning is not just in the economic order. The scandal, the stumbling block which Jesus presents to his contemporaries is that on the one hand he simply ignores the lines which every society draws to separate the good from the bad and accepts freely into his company those on the wrong side of every line — whether the prostitute from the streets or the rich and corrupt tax-collector from his mansion; and that on the other hand he confronts them all in his own person with the actual claim and offer of the kingly rule of God. As the story of Zacchaeus illustrates, no one can come under that rule without a conversion, which means a total break with both personal and 'structural' injustice. But the scandal is Jesus himself. The presence of the kingdom is the presence of Jesus himself. Parables and 'mighty works' can only offer the possibility, never the guaranteed certainty that men's eyes will be opened to see the presence of the reign of God in this man Jesus the son of Mary. The secret of the kingdom is hidden as it is unveiled.

Finally parable and mighty work lead up to that event which is both the supreme parable and the supreme mighty work — the crucifixion of Jesus as an excommunicated criminal. Here — therefore — is the point where the paradox of veiling and unveiling reaches its climax; here Jesus is either the corner stone or the stumbling block. The cross is either the power of God and the wisdom of God — in fact the reign of God actually present — or else it is scandal and folly. It is to those who are called, called by God not by themselves, that the crucified Lord is the presence of the kingdom of God in wisdom and power (I Cor. 1:18–25).

Let me pause here and, in the light of this review, make some negative statements and put some questions. Why, to begin with, was the liberal Christianity of the 1920s so eager to separate the Kingdom of God from the name of Jesus? Why was that era so eager to talk about the coming of the kingdom but so very reluctant to speak of the second coming of Jesus? Why so ready with the prayer 'Thy Kingdom come' but so reluctant to pray 'Come, Lord Jesus'? Why was the introduction of the name of Jesus seen as something divisive and sectarian, while the message of the kingdom was seen as all-inclusive? Why was Paul so freely accused in that period of having introduced a message different from the simple Gospel of Jesus and the Kingdom? 'Jesus preached the kingdom of God; Paul preached a religion about Jesus' was the constant charge against the apostle. Surely a candid review of the evidence shows that the accusation is misplaced. Jesus did indeed preach the kingdom, but the only thing that made his preaching news was that the kingdom was present in himself. Faithfulness to the mission and message of Jesus absolutely required that the early Church should have Jesus as the centre of their gospel. If they had simply preached about the kingdom of God there would have been no gospel. The *news* is that 'the kingdom of God' is no longer merely a theological phrase. There is now a name and a human face. This is why there is a gospel: the reign of God *has* drawn near, and we can speak of what we have seen and heard and handled (I John 1:1-2). The apostle would have denied the central message of Jesus if he had *not* made that shift of language from 'kingdom' to 'Jesus'.

Looking back on the kind of missionary writing which culminated in the 'Laymen's Enquiry' of 1932 it is easy to see — with hindsight — that the language of the kingdom was used to effect a quiet transfer from the Gospel about Jesus to a programme based on the ideology of the progressive capitalism of the United States at that point in time. That shift is easily detected from our point of vantage fifty years later. It is less easy to be aware of similar shifts in our own time. We can see that the alliance between the Christian mission and the expansion of capitalism — even at its best — was illegitimate. In relation to our own time it is equally necessary to recognise that the language of the kingdom of God can easily degenerate into mere ideology if the name and the fact of Jesus is not kept right at the centre. Only so is the message of the kingdom of God Gospel and not ideology.

If we have to insist that there must be no separation of the message of the kingdom from the name of Jesus, how is it with regard to the relation between the message of the kingdom and the existence and growth of the Church? As an approach to this question I would like to continue our use of the Lucan narrative into the opening chapters of Acts. At the beginning of Luke's second volume we read that the apostles asked Jesus:

> 'Lord, will you at this time restore the kingdom to Israel?' He said to them, 'It is not for you to know times or seasons which the Father has fixed by his own authority. But you shall receive power when

the Holy Spirit has come upon you; and you shall
be my witnesses in Jerusalem and in all Judea and
Samaria and to the end of the earth.'

Those who ask the question are those who have
been chosen and called to see the risen Lord and to
believe. The risen Lord did not appear (as is often said)
to believers; he appeared 'not to all the people but to
us who were chosen by God as witnesses' (Acts 10:41).
It was not that they saw the risen Lord because they
were believers; they became believers because they were
chosen to be witnesses of the risen Lord. Now they are
believers. The appalling experiences of Jesus' betrayal,
condemnation, dereliction and death are behind them.
They are the first to be called to recognise in the crucified Lord the presence of the power and the wisdom
of God. They do believe. Therefore it is natural and
reasonable that they should go back to the original
message with which the ministry began — the message
of the coming of the kingdom — and ask: Is the message now to be proved true? Can we expect the manifest coming of the reign of God now? It is a reasonable
question.

The answer of Jesus is in the double form of warning and promise. It is first of all warning: it is not for
you to know times or seasons which the Father has
fixed by his own authority. The kingdom is, quite simply, the reign of *God*. This is so fundamental that it is
constantly forgotten. We are not dealing here with a
programme, a campaign, a promotional 'drive' for which
the techniques of high-pressure salesmanship or mili-
tary planning would be appropriate. Nor are we en-
gaged in the support of a 'good cause' about which it
is possible for us to be optimistic or pessimistic. The

first kind of misunderstanding is characteristic of those who have worldly power and wealth behind them; it is abundantly illustrated in material emanating from the American 'Church Growth' agencies. The second is characteristic of those who are in a weak position from a worldly point of view; it is very pathetically illustrated in the anxiety with which church people in Britain are inclined to look at the findings of public opinion surveys and the comments of sociologists. Whether in its 'optimistic' or 'pessimistic' form, this way of thinking about the Gospel is surely wide of the mark. It is not possible to be either optimistic or pessimistic about the sovereignty of God! It is simply a fact. The question about which everyone has to enquire is the question: am I living in total faithfulness, trust and loving obedience to him who is the sovereign? The sharp words of Jesus have to be heeded in every situation — whether the temptation is to a worldly optimism or to a worldly pessimism. Our attention is directed to God himself. He alone is the king. What is called for in us is a total trust which — whether in success or in failure — simply places all its hope in him; which accepts the promise: Fear not, little flock, it is your Father's good pleasure to give you the kingdom.

I think that this is a warning which has to be heeded as we take the theme of the kingdom as a clue for missionary thinking. There is a very easy but fatal shift that can take place by which the language of the Bible, which always points to the personal presence and action of God, is converted into language which points to programmes of our own. I have in mind, for example, such great passages as we find in Psalms 145 and 146: God is faithful in all his words and gracious in all his deeds; the Lord upholds all who are falling, and raises up all who are bowed down. . . . The Lord is just in all his ways and kind in all his doings. . . . He fulfils the desire of all who fear him (Ps. 145:17–19). The Lord executes justice for the oppressed and gives food to the hungry. He sets the prisoners free and opens the eyes of the blind. The Lord lifts up those who are bowed down; the Lord loves the righteous (Ps. 146:7–8). When this language is translated into abstract nouns — justice, liberation and satisfaction of basic human needs — a subtle but profound change has been made. The biblical language is totally centred in the reality of the living God — his faithfulness and kindness. The other kind of language leads quickly into an ideology which is centred entirely in one's expectations about the possibilities of political action. The biblical language has been for so long (and especially in our western culture) interpreted in a purely private and pietistic sense divorced from the realities and the obligations of political life, that a correction was urgently needed. But in making this correction it is important that one does not lose that which is central to the biblical witness — the formidable reality of God who is alone sovereign in his kingdom. The fact that the Melbourne theme has been formulated as a prayer addressed to God will, I believe, safeguard its further development against this deviation.

The answer of Jesus to the question of the disciples is, in the second place, a *promise*. 'You shall receive power when the Holy Spirit has come upon you, and you shall be my witnesses. . . .' The first point to be noted is that this is a promise, not a command. Witness is not a burden laid upon the Church. It is not part of the law. It is gospel, gift, promise. We misinterpret the whole thrust of the New Testament when we convert this into a law, a burden laid upon the consciences of Christians. There is a profound inner necessity which leads Christians to bear witness to Jesus and Paul's letters bear ample evidence of this. But neither Paul nor any of the other New Testament writers can be found laying the duty of witness as a burden upon the consciences of their readers. Failure to observe this point, I think, has had grievous consequences in the life of the Church. What is given here is not a command but a promise.

How is the promise related to the question? The question is about the Kingdom; the promise is about that which is the foretaste, the first-fruit, the *arrabon* of the Kingdom — namely the gift of the Spirit. The word *arrabon* which is (I am told) still used in colloquial Arabic, expresses vividly what is otherwise expressed in such metaphors as 'foretaste' and 'firstfruit'. An *arrabon* is a payment which is, on the one hand, solid cash which can be spent like any other money, and, on the other hand, is a sign and pledge of full payment to come. It is not mere verbal promise. It is real cash. Yet its significance is far more than its actual cash value; it is the assurance of much more to come. The Holy Spirit is such an *arrabon* of the Kingdom. It is, on the one hand, a real foretaste of the love and joy and peace which are the very substance of God's rule. But — on the other hand — it is not yet the fulness of these things. It is the solid pledge which gives assurance that the fulness is coming. And this is what constitutes the witness. It is not the lantern which a traveller in the dark carries in his hand; it is the glow

on his face which reflects the coming dawn. It is pure
gift. It is not an accomplishment of the one who bears
witness but rather a gift which comes from beyond
him and so directs men's attention away from the bearer
to the source of the gift — to the light in the eastern
sky. In this sense one must say that the Church is not
the author of the witness; it is not that the Church
bears witness and that the Spirit helps the Church to
do so. This kind of language completely misses the
point. The point is that the Church is the place where
the Spirit is present as witness. The witness is thus
not an accomplishment of the Church but a promise
to the Church.

The Lucan story goes on to recount the fulfilment
of the promise on the day of Pentecost. Here, one may
say, the mission begins; but it does not begin with a
decision *by* the Church on the basis of a command
which it has received. It begins with something which
happens *to* the Church, something which it is immediately called upon to explain. People of every race and
language come running to ask 'What is going on here?',
and the Church is required to answer. The first Christian sermon is preached not on the initiative of the
preacher but in answer to questions by the people. It
is already part of a conversation, a dialogue. And the
answer which Peter gives to the question begins with
eschatology; the 'last days' have dawned and the presence of the Spirit is the sign that this is so. And from
this beginning at the end, the preacher has to work
backwards to those events which constitute the dawn-
ing of the last days — the life and death and resurrection of Jesus of Nazareth.

Nor is this first sermon unique. A study of Acts will

show that the normal context in which the gospel is preached is the same; a question is asked which needs an answer, and the question is prompted by recognition of a prior reality — the reality of the presence of the Spirit. It is the Spirit who takes the initiatives: the Church has to learn to follow. Sometimes it follows very reluctantly, as in the case of Peter and Cornelius. In that story (Acts 10 and 11) Peter shows no evidence whatever of being aware of an obligation to share the Gospel with the household of a pagan soldier. He is taken there in spite of his protestations. He is directly questioned by Cornelius. He begins to tell the story of Jesus and, before he has finished, the matter is taken out of his hands. Cornelius and his household have been taken up into that same experience of the presence and power of God which had overwhelmed the apostles at Pentecost. Peter can only follow where the Spirit has led.

So it is throughout the book which might well have been entitled 'The Acts of the Spirit'. The initiative is with the Spirit; the Church follows. On the one hand the Spirit is not domesticated within the Church but leads the Church in sovereign freedom. On the other hand the Spirit is not separated from the Church, for the Spirit's work is to lead men and women to confess Jesus as Lord, and the Church is the place where that confession is made. On the one hand the Spirit (the *arrabon* of the Kingdom) is constantly creating and recreating the Church. On the other hand the Church, which is not the author or controller of the Spirit's witness to the Kingdom, is the place where that witness is given and acknowledged. Because of the work of the Spirit, therefore, the Church may become a sign of the Kingdom.

This picture of the relations between the terms Spirit, Witness and Church is confirmed when we turn to the Johannine discourses (John 14 to 17). Here the Spirit is the one promised to the Church, when it faithfully follows Jesus, to be the very presence of God himself (14:15f). He is the one promised to the Church when it is rejected and condemned by the world, to be the advocate who bears witness to Jesus — speaking the words which the Church does not know how to speak (15:16f; cf. Mark 13:9–11). He is the one promised to the Church to go before it in its encounter with the world — the advocate for the prosecution, confuting the world's most fundamental notions (16:7–11). And he is the one promised to the Church to guide the Church into the fulness of the truth, truth which the Church cannot receive immediately but only as the Spirit takes what belongs to the Father (and therefore also to Jesus) and shows it to the Church — thus enabling the Church to interpret what is to come (16:12–15).

How, in the light of this, are we to state the relation between Church and Kingdom? On the one hand, the Church is warned that the Kingdom is God's Kingdom. In regard to the time and manner of its coming the Church can exercise no kind of control but must place its trust simply and absolutely in the Father. It is not the Church's 'cause' or 'programme'. It is, quite simply, God's reign. What is promised to the Church is the *arrabon* of the kingdom, the Spirit whose presence *is* the witness to the kingdom, and who, in sovereign freedom, goes before the Church, leads the Church into the fulness of the truth, achieves the communication which the Church's own words cannot achieve, keeps the Church within the love and power of the Father, and brings ever new peoples to the confession of Jesus as Lord.

It is by a firm grasp of the New Testament teaching about the Spirit that we shall come to a right understanding of the relation between Church and Kingdom. We will not come to a right understanding by simply trying to find a middle way between two obvious errors — the error of identifying the Church with the kingdom so that everything is concentrated on the growth and prosperity of the Church, and the error of separating the Church from the preaching of the kingdom so that we are left with a mere programme. The Holy Spirit, the real presence of God in the company of believers, is given as the veritable foretaste and first fruit of the kingdom and therefore as the witness of the reality of the Kingdom. For this witness of the Spirit the words and the deeds and the corporate life of the fellowship may indeed provide the *locus* and the occasion. But the work of the Spirit is always his work, always something which is beyond anything that can be explained as the work of the Church. The Spirit furnishes the Church with varied gifts distributed among its many members — gifts which can build up the life of the body precisely because they are so different from one another. But the deployment of these gifts (if one may use the phrase) is the work of the Spirit himself. The strategy is not in the hands of the Church. There is no simple line from the words and deeds of the Church to the manifestation of God's kingdom. If a man or woman comes to see that the cross of Jesus is not a folly and a scandal but is the very power and wisdom of God, then that is always a miracle, a supernatural work of the Spirit of God himself. The human words and deeds of the Church will have provided — here and there — the occasion for that work; but the work itself is always a work of the Spirit, a miracle that goes beyond human contriving.

The point that I am making may be put both negatively and positively. Negatively, the Church may never equate the success of its own strategies with the victory of God's kingdom. Positively, the only hermeneutic of the message of the Kingdom is the presence of a community in which the foretaste of the kingdom, the Spirit, is already present. Negatively, then, every attempt to put 'Church Growth' in the centre of attention; everything which makes it appear that we are essentially interested only in the growth and welfare of the Church, and in the world only as contributing to this is a betrayal of the kingdom and makes the Church appear as a self-regarding society which stands between ordinary people and the vision of the kingdom. On the other hand, apart from a living community in which there is already a foretaste of the reality of the Kingdom, a present experience of its joy and freedom, the preaching of the kingdom becomes mere ideology. We have seen this happen in the past where 'kingdom' has been separated from 'church' in missionary thinking. When abstract nouns replace the biblical language about God's just and loving rule, this is what happens — and the same is true whether these nouns are such as were popular fifty years ago ('social progress', 'civilisation', etc.) or such as are popular now ('liberation', 'justice', etc.). The *content* of the preaching of the Kingdom can never be any such concepts; it can only be Jesus himself, incarnate, crucified and risen. The *hermeneutic* can only be the living reality of a community in which the first fruits of the Kingdom are already being enjoyed and shared. This will be a community which shares fully in solidarity with the suffering of the oppressed and therefore shares the secret of Christ's victory over death and the hope of the completion of that victory at the end. The whole of the eighth chapter of Romans is a picture of such a community, sharing in the tribulation of Jesus and therefore sharing also in the assurance, hope and joy of his victory. Such a community will be the living hermeneutic of the message of the Kingdom which it preaches. There can be no other.

III

The Theme in the Context of Today's Mission

What kind of Church will it be which lives in and by the prayer 'Your Kingdom come' in the context of today's world?

1. It will be a church which is in the world but not of the world. That over-used phrase has been replaced in recent talk by the phrase 'a church for others', and we can accept that description provided that the preposition 'for' is rightly understood. It has to be understood Christologically. The Church is to be 'for' others in the same sense in which Christ was and is 'for' the world. In the light of the previous discussion we may be more precise and say 'a church which is a sign of the Kingdom in the same sense in which Jesus was a sign of the Kingdom.' Clearly this means a church which does not exist for itself or for what it can offer to its members; a church which is not offering personal salvation to its members apart from the salvation which God offers to the whole world, apart from the destiny of the nations and the cosmos. It means a church which is a credible sign of the *malkuth yahweh*, the just and loving rule of God over his whole creation and his whole family.

When the Christian Church was first launched into the life of the eastern Roman Empire it found itself surrounded by many religious societies which claimed to offer personal salvation to their members through a variety of teaching and disciplines. Several Greek words were in use to describe such societies *(thiasos, heranos,* etc.). As private religious societies they enjoyed the protection of the state. If the Christian Church had seen itself in this way it would have been content to use these names and could have availed itself of this protection. But, although (for example) critics like Celsus described the Church in this way, these words were never used by the Church to describe itself. Of the two words used in the Septuagint to translate the Hebrew names for the whole congregation of Israel, the word *synagogos,* already used by the Jewish diaspora, was avoided and the word *ecclesia* was almost universally adopted — the word which in normal secular use referred to the public assembly of all the citizens gathered to discuss and settle the public affairs of the city. In other words, the early Church did not see itself as a private religious society competing with others to offer personal salvation to its members; it saw itself as a movement launched into the public life of the world, challenging the *cultus publicus* of the Empire, claiming the allegiance of all without exception.

This universal claim was being made by communities which were — from the point of view of *realpolitik* — insignificant. When one remembers what these communities were in relation to the society of the time, there is something staggering about the words that Paul uses. In the Letter to the Colossians, after speaking of Christ as the cosmic head of all creation, he

continues without any break to speak of him as 'the
head of the body, the Church'. In the very similar passage of Ephesians we read that God has put all things
under the feet of Christ 'and made him the head over
all things for the church which is his body' (Col. 1:18;
Eph. 1:22f). The claim for universal sovereignty is made
in the face of the overwhelming powers that rule the
world and the Church is identified as the body whose
head is this cosmic sovereign. The Church was on a
collision course with the established powers, and for
three centuries paid the price for this stupendous claim.

Then came the event which the Seer of Patmos could
not have anticipated — the conversion and baptism of
the Emperor. It is fashionable to the present time to
speak of this as a disaster for the Church. In our present historical situation, when we struggle to free ourselves from the clinging remnants of the Constantinian
era, this is understandable. We are painfully aware of
the consequences of that conversion; for centuries the
Church was allied with the established power, sanc-
tioned and even wielded the sword, lost its critical relation to the ruling authorities. But what should the
Church of the fourth century have done? Should it have
refused to baptise the Emperor on the ground that it
is better for the spiritual health of the Church to be
persecuted than to be in the seats of power? The discussion is unrealistic and futile. We have to accept that
as a matter of fact the first great attempt to translate
the universal claim of Christ into political terms was
the Constantinian settlement. Christ as Pantocrator
took on the lineaments of the Roman Emperor. We
cannot go behind that; we have to live with its consequences and learn from them. These consequences are

familiar to us. When the whole of society (except the Jews) is baptised and the Church is the spiritual arm of the establishment, the critical rôle of the Church devolves upon separate bodies — the monks, the radical sectarian groups, the millenarian movements on the fringes of the Church.

But in the last three centuries western Christendom has moved into a new situation. A new ideology has replaced the Christian vision as the *cultus publicus* of western Christendom. It is the vision which dawned in that remarkable experience which those who shared it called 'the enlightenment'. It was a new vision of the world as totally explicable by means of the new tools for rational analysis which were being developed, and of man as the bearer of the meaning of his own history, and of the future as an ever-expanding mastery of man's reason over nature leading to a golden age of total rationality and total mastery over all the powers that threaten man. The word 'enlightenment' (reminiscent of the experience of the Buddha) expresses the quality of this vision. Light had dawned and darkness was being banished. The previous centuries during which Europe had been christianised, were darkness. The rest of the world (with the possible exception of China) was darkness. Now the light had dawned; western man had only to walk in that light, spread that light, and all the nations would have fellowship one with another. The 'blood of Jesus' (I Jn. 1:7) was not required.

At the risk of extreme over-simplification one would have to say that the Church failed to challenge this new *cultus publicus* effectively and took the road which the early Church had refused; it retreated into the private sector. The new vision was allowed to control public life. The 'enlightened' world carried its message, its science and technology, and its masterful relation to the world, into every part of the globe. The Christian vision was allowed to illuminate personal and domestic life, but not to challenge the vision that controlled the public sector. The Church took on more and more the shape which the early Church had refused: it became a group of societies which were seen as offering spiritual consolation and the hope of personal salvation to those who chose to belong.

The change can be illustrated most vividly by looking at what happened to the teaching of history in schools and universities. From the time of Augustine and Orosius up to the eighteenth century, world history was taught on the basis of that vision of history which is embodied in the Bible. The Bible is in the form of a universal history and its vision of the meaning and end of universal history derives from the events which are associated with the names of Abraham, Isaac and Jacob, Moses, Jesus. The new vision of universal history was quite different. It derived from the new experience of mastery over nature through science and technology. It saw man as the bearer of the meaning of his own history. From this point of view the names and events of which the Bible speaks can have only a very marginal significance. Consequently the teaching of history now takes two different forms. In the secular classroom 'world history' is taught in terms of the new vision; in the 'religious instruction' classes the biblical history is still taught, but it is taught rather as a series of parables illuminating the problems of personal life. This is the situation with which we now have to

deal. Nor is it simply our local situation here in Western Europe. The missionary expansion of the western
churches during the past two centuries has been — obviously — determined by what was happening at the
'home base'. The 'light' which modern missionaries
brought to Asia and Africa was not just the light of
the gospel. It was a fusion of these two lights: such
words as 'civilisation', 'development' and 'technical as-
sistance', which have been freely bracketed with 'evangelism' in the recent history of missions, remind us that
this is no mere domestic problem. There are indeed a
few small corners of the world where something like
the 'Christendom' pattern still prevails. A visitor to
Western Samoa or Tonga has the impression that he
is in such a situation; but this is exceptional. The
Christendom era is behind us. Around us is the situation I have tried to describe, where Christianity has
become a *cultus privatus* tolerated within a society
whose *cultus publicus* has been shaped by the vision
of the Enlightenment. Before us is the new task of
developing a pattern of churchmanship which can
credibly represent Christ's claim to universal dominion
over all the life of the world without attempting to
follow again the Constantinian road. That is our task
now. What is the proper contemporary equivalent of
the vision of Christ as Pantocrator? How can the
Church become a credible sign to all peoples of every
kind, a sign of the kingship of God as it is set forth in
the Bible — a kingship which *offers* the fulness of life,
peace, justice and holiness; and at the same time *requires* the total obedience of every creature?

    The only possible answer to this question is that
the Church can become such a sign insofar as, and

only insofar as, her life is assimilated to the life of Jesus who was himself the only sign given of the Kingdom, Jesus himself the crucified King who bears in his risen body the marks of his passion (John 20:19–23). Only the Church which bears those marks can be recognisable as the body of Christ and recognisable therefore as a sign of the Kingdom. To spell this out more explicitly: the Church can be a sign of the Kingdom insofar as it follows Jesus in steadfastly challenging the powers of evil in the life of the world by accepting total solidarity with those who are the victims of those powers; insofar as, by accepting in its own life the weight of the world's wrong it exposes and judges the wrongdoers in the act of saving both them and their victims.

2. Let me try now to come a little closer to contemporary realities and to spell out what might be the implications of this answer for our churches in this western world.

I think that the first implication must be a radical break with the ideology of capitalism. Our timid compromise with this ideology has persisted too long. The ideology of the free market can only be accepted by a church which has retreated into the private sector. The free market system works by means of the unremitting stimulation of consumer demand among those who have the purchasing power to make that demand effective. Translated into biblical language, this is to say that it works by the unremitting stimulation of gluttony among those who already have enough. It necessarily channels resources into the production of goods according to the demand of the relatively prosperous and not according to the need of the poor. In every democratic society which has adopted the principle of the free market, it has been found necessary almost at once to use the powers of Government to prevent the limitless exploitation of the weak and defenceless. It can be reasonably argued that in certain circumstances a 'mixed economy' in which there is a balance between the power of the free market and the power of the State, is the best available system. But acceptance of the *ideology* of the free market is, I think, forbidden for a Christian. It is important to say this just because its power is so all-pervasive.

On the other hand, this break with the ideology of capitalism should not lead the Church to a new alliance with the ideology of Marxism. It is necessary to say this in the present context. The Marxist analysis of the working of the free market clearly contains a large amount of truth, as does Karl Marx's criticism of the ideology of capitalism. Moreover Marxism has gained a new credibility in the past twenty years for understandable reasons. The creation of a vast new international currency system at the Bretton Woods Conference at the end of the last war opened the way for an unprecedented explosion of economic activity throughout that part of the world which came within its scope (the 'free world'). Multi-national business corporations developed on a gigantic scale which dwarfed the power of all but the largest nation-states. But, whereas within each nation-state governments had early assumed powers to curb the working of the free market so as to protect the defenceless, there were and are no transnational governmental agencies powerful enough to do the same thing on the world scale. The

successive UNCTAD meetings, and the discussions
about a New International Economic Order, have all
failed to generate enough political will among the great
powers to curb the gigantic power of the transnational
corporations. Consequently the conditions of early capitalism which were the context of Marx's writings are
now being produced afresh on the global level. It is
therefore very natural that Marxism should appear as
the only interpretation of events which is credible to
those of the poorer nations which have become the
external proletariat of the western world.

No serious Christian, I suppose, advocates an un-
conditional alliance with Marxism. But the utopian ele-
ment in Marxism, the vision of a classless society where
the State has 'withered away' and there is no such
thing as coercive authority, does greatly attract Christians in our time. There is a proper place in Christian
political thinking for what is often called a utopia,
understood as a middle-distance objective which can
command wide allegiance and can direct political judgment. But when such a utopia becomes the ultimate
goal beside which everything else is relativised very
serious consequences follow. The vision, which is a
human construct, becomes an idol and becomes therefore an instrument of dehumanisation. The idol is put
in the place which ought to be occupied by actual men
and women suffering now under the power of evil. The
human being who is living and suffering now is mar-
ginalised by the vision of a future society which he will
never be able to see or enjoy. Compassion is rejected
because it might serve to keep the present system going
and therefore delay the arrival of the new world. The
reality of God's present gift of grace and strength in

the midst of trouble is denied. In the name of a justice to be achieved in the future, the justification which is offered now is rejected. Life becomes a struggle with no place for joy, a desert without manna, and everything in the present is sacrificed to the dream of a future which those now living will never see. There is something pathetic about the way in which Christians fall so easily for this illusion. I can not forget the WCC Assembly at Uppsala, sitting in rapt attention while the singer Piet Sieger sang 'Pie in the sky when you die', and receiving it as though it were some kind of new gospel. This kind of utopianism not only mocks people with sheer illusion; it also robs them of that joy which Jesus promised to those who follow him on the way of the cross, joy precisely in the midst of tribulation because it is a sharing here and now in the firstfruits of his resurrection victory.

If, then, we must avoid commitment to either of these ideologies, how can we indicate the direction in which the Church must go. What does it mean to accept the commission of Jesus 'As the Father sent me, so I send you'? What exactly is the force of that 'as'? What direction does it indicate? When it was clear that Israel had rejected Jesus' message of the Kingdom, there were — humanly speaking — two ways which he might have taken. One was that of the Zealots; he could have put himself at the head of those who were seeking national liberation by force. There were obviously the makings of a revolution in the contemporary situation. Jesus could have become part of that movement which ended forty years later at Masada. The other possible route was that of the Essenes, also leading to the desert shores of the Dead Sea. He could have withdrawn with his disciples to form a community of prayer, waiting for the kingdom which God alone can bring.

What Jesus did was something different from either of these. He rode right into the centre of political power at the moment of maximum political expectation and challenged the powers with a kingly claim which had nothing in common with the kind of claims that were represented in Caiaphas and Pontius Pilate. In defenceless vulnerability he challenged the reign of evil and by doing so took upon himself the full force of its onslaught. In doing so he achieved a victory over the power of evil which was both hidden and revealed — hidden from the perception of the practitioners of *realpolitik*, revealed to the faith of those who were committed to him as the foretaste of a total victory promised at the end.

However many may be the difficulties in seeking to apply this model to the contemporary tasks of the Church, there can surely be no doubt that this is the model. It is to a church which follows this way that the promise is given (and constantly confirmed in experience) of the presence of the Spirit as the foretaste of the victory of God's reign and the witness of its reality. To follow this way requires not only courage and the willingness to face suffering and rejection, but also discernment in order to recognise those situations where the reign of God is being contradicted by the powers of evil. In the great parable of the Last Judgment (Matt. 25:31–46) those who are condemned are those who failed to discern in the situations where they were the presence of the suffering of the Christ. On the other hand those who were moved by compassion

for the suffering of their neighbours were in fact the
recipients of blessing; in their compassion they were
meeting Christ himself.

The word 'compassion' is not very much used in
contemporary discussion of the mission of the Church.
There are reasons for this — good and bad. The good
reason is that the word has often been used to justify
a quietist attitude to political issues, a recommenda-
tion to endure injustice rather than to change unjust
structures. On this two things are to be said. On the
one hand, where Christians are in a position to exercise
pressure for the changing of unjust structures by political means and fail to do so, they are guilty of dis-
obedience. The privatisation of religion in contemporary
western culture has allowed Christians to think that
Christian obedience stops short at the boundaries of
personal and domestic life and does not include political action. This is a denial of the fundamental Christian faith in the universal lordship of Christ. On the
other hand, there are situations where existing unjust
structures cannot immediately be changed by any fore-
seeable combination of powers except for the worst. In
such situations compassion, sharing in the suffering of
the victim, is the primary form of Christian response.
Out of compassion will spring such actions as are possible to bring relief, but the compassion is primary.

There are also bad reasons for rejecting compassion, and these have already been referred to. There is
a false utopianism which drains the present of all
meaning and invests everything in a future which is
supposed to be just ahead of us. For those who are
gripped by this anything which makes the present more
tolerable is to be rejected because it delays the coming

of the future. Thus the living human beings who suffer and die long before Utopia arrives are exploited for the sake of an illusion. Against this as against everything which exploits man in the name of an idea, the Christian must be a firm dissenter.

To sum up: the Church cannot accept the privatisation which has been its normal position since the Enlightenment. It cannot allow itself to be regarded as a society existing for the religious and other needs of its members. It must challenge the contemporary *cultus publicus,* and this means a radical break with the dominant ideology of capitalism. But in making this break it must not fall into a similar alliance with the ideology of Marxism. It must pursue the course which is set for it by its Lord. It must be a sign and foretaste of God's universal kingdom, in the way and only in the way that Jesus was the sign. It must make clear always and everywhere its claim upon the total life of the world, and yet not make this claim in the Constantinian manner. It must therefore find a style of living and speaking which holds together in tension the accepting, blessing and fostering of the whole life of the world with the challenging and exposing of it in the light of the Cross. Such a style of living and speaking can only mean that the Church itself bears the marks of the cross in its own life. The risen body of Christ is recognisable by the scars of the passion (John 20:20). Only so is it also the place where the Spirit is present to release men and women from the grip of evil (John 20:22f).

3. Let me now go on to ask what will be the implications of such a vision for the structures of the Church? From our Constantinian past, and from the experi-

ences of the break-up of the Constantinian settlement, we have inherited three kinds of structure.

(a) There is the territorial parish and diocese, an obvious relic of the 'Christendom' era. Here the entire resident population of an area is seen as being the responsibility of one unit of the Church's organisation.

(b) There is the 'gathered congregation' consisting of those who have chosen to form such a congregation. Its members may come from several parishes, but they are committed to one another as a congregation.

(c) There is a salaried professional class of men and women, comparable to such professional groups as lawyers, doctors and civil servants, who provide the leadership for parishes and congregations.

The first of these structures is a clear relic of the 'Christendom' era. The second is a structural consequence of the privatisation of religion in our culture. The third is a carry-over from the first to the second. What we have now to seek are forms of Church and ministry which neither draw men and women out of the world into a private society, nor seek to dominate the world through controlling centres of power, but enable men and women to function within the secular life of the world in ways which reflect the reality of Christ's passion and thereby make the reality of Christ's resurrection credible to the victims of the world's wrong.

In the effort to meet the changing situation of our contemporary culture various new structural forms have appeared and play a part in the mission of the Church. Three of these may be mentioned.

(d) Programme agencies of various kinds which exist to carry on work in the fields of evangelism, education and social and political action. These agencies may be related to a particular denomination, or they may be ecumenical. In any case they are programme agencies and not 'local churches' in any definition of that term.

(e) 'Sector Ministries'. By this is meant people, normally ordained ministers, who are related not to a 'local church' but to some sector of secular life such as industry, education or healing.

(f) 'Para-churches'. I use this term without any negative intention to describe the great and growing number of groups which are formed on the basis of a common vision for the Church, or of a common concern about Christian action in the world, and which meet apart from the traditional gatherings of the 'local church' for worship. Members of these groups are frequently, but not necessarily, also members of local churches. The largest and most significant group in this category consists of the 'base communities' which have become a very rapidly growing movement especially in the Latin countries of Europe and Latin America. In many of these communities the celebration of the sacraments is a normal part of their meeting, and they are therefore difficult to distinguish from 'local congregations' in the traditional sense.

Each of these structural developments is playing an important part in enabling the Church to penetrate areas of secular life from which the privatised religion of western culture has been largely excluded. They are important growing points for the mission of the Church. Their weaknesses arise precisely at the point of their separation from the local congregation.

Programme agencies apparently had their first effective development in the United States of America.

In fact it seems to be the case that the phenomenon of denominationalism is a product of this development which has spread from America to the rest of western Christendom. Before the rise of the mission and educational agencies in the early nineteenth century there was hardly anything of what we would call a denominational structure binding together local congregations of the various traditions. The General Assembly of the Presbyterian Church had — apparently — no funds of its own until well into the nineteenth century. In England the development of powerful denominational boards is a very recent development, and the ecumenical agencies of the national and world councils of churches have come later still. These agencies do express the Church's concern for the whole secular life of the nation and the world. They thus witness to something which has been denied or obscured by the privatisation of religion. Their weakness is that they have no visible relation to the life of worship and fellowship which constitutes the life of the local congregation. These agencies and the life of the congregations do not mutually correct one another. Consequently, on the one hand, the local congregation is not challenged to remember that it exists for the sake of its neighbourhood; it is rather encouraged to exist as a society for its own members because the wider responsibilities are carried by another agency. On the other hand the work of the agency is not seen to spring right out of the life of worship and fellowship in the Gospel. It is not seen as an overspill of a charismatic experience. It appears simply as a programme, and those who have to bear responsibility for its work are almost compelled to become representatives of the law rather than of the gospel. There is, in fact, a notoriously wide gap between the thinking of the local congregation and the thinking that governs the work of many of these agencies. The Gospel which is celebrated in the local congregation and the programme which is carried out by the agency appear to be unrelated to each other. And this is fatal for the witness of the Church. By contrast, when a local congregation is deeply involved in the wrongs and sufferings of its neighbourhood, when worship in the sanctuary leads straight out into action in the street, then it is possible for the outsider to see that the one springs from the other and he is led to ask about the spring from which faith, hope and love flow. The compassion and the action of the church members then become signs that point beyond themselves.

Something similar must be said about the 'sector ministries'. However, here some distinctions must be made. Chaplaincies to schools, universities and hospitals have been in existence for a very long time and in these places the chaplain is really the minister of a believing congregation which worships in the chapel of the school or hospital. This is a different situation from that of those who are assigned to work in industry, local government and similar spheres. Here the chaplain is largely on his own. He does not visibly represent a community in which the joy and fellowship of the Gospel is a living reality. It is hard for him to avoid being seen simply as the bearer of a message, of a programme. He is tempted to move into the situation where he is the bearer of 'solutions' to 'problems'. Industrial chaplains, in England at least, are very deeply involved in wrestling with the ethical problems of modern industry and are inclined to distance themselves

from the traditional local congregations. This is completely understandable. The piety represented in these
congregations has often very little to do with the ethical
issues with which a man in industry must deal. And
if a Christian has nothing to say about these ethical
issues, he has surely no place in industry. But it is not
difficult to see what is lacking in this set-up. The Gospel is never simply an answer to an ethical problem.
It is the gift of a new life in which all things are seen
in a new perspective and in which one has courage
and hope and compassion for living among problems
which one cannot immediately solve. This gift is always a supernatural gift of the Holy Spirit, but the
human condition is the presence of a congregation of
those who are living by this gift. That is the only possible hermeneutic for the gospel that the chaplain has
to deliver, and in the typical situation of an industrial
chaplain it is lacking. By contrast I have seen situations where a local congregation with its minister was
deeply involved in the problems and the agonies of the
industries around them, and had become a place where
the people involved in these problems found understanding and acceptance and hope. In such situations
not only is there a real witness to the lordship of Christ
over the world of industry, but also the local congregation is challenged to leave its private ghetto and become more recognisable as a sign and firstfruit of God's
reign over all things.

When we come to speak of the development of 'para-
churches' we enter a different area of discussion. These
groups at their best *are* the local congregation in its
most vivid form — taking 'locality' here to refer not only
or primarily to geographical closeness of residence but

to the sharing of a common 'place' in the secular life of the world. The Medellin Conference of the Latin American bishops spoke of the Basic Community as the 'primary and fundamental ecclesial nucleus' and it is clear that here the intention is that these communities shall be integrated into the life of the parish so that the parish is seen as 'a confederation of basal ecclesial communities' (International Review of Mission, No. 271, pp. 235ff). As thus interpreted these communities are a dynamic way of opening up the traditional local congregation for a much deeper involvement with the life of the world. They represent an immense movement of renewal in the Church. However there is also another kind of 'para-church' which is characterised by the slogan 'Let us leave the Church in order to be the Church'. This has been the slogan of sectarians in every age, and the ecclesiastical scene is littered with the debris which such movements leave behind in the next generation. There is bound to be tension between a new vision of the Church as it should be and the reality of the Church as it is. The most creative results follow when the tension can be held without snapping. This does seem to be happening in the experience of the 'base communities' in many parts of the world. But there are also communities formed around one particular and partial vision of the task of the Church and when these separate themselves from the wider fellowship of the worshipping congregation, they very quickly move into new and oppressive forms of legalism.

It is the Church as a whole which has to be the hermeneutic of the Gospel, and the question which has to be asked about these and other movements of fresh outreach into the world is whether they contribute to the renewal and re-shaping of the life of the ordinary local congregation in every place. And the question which has to be put to every local congregation is the question whether it is a credible sign of God's reign in justice and mercy over the whole of life, whether it is an open fellowship whose concerns are as wide as the concerns of humanity, whether it cares for its neighbours in a way which reflects and springs out of God's care for them, whether its common life is recognisable as a foretaste of the blessing which God intends for the whole human family.

It seems to me clear that the development of this kind of congregational life will call for congregations which are related to the different sectors of the secular world as well as those which are related to the geographical areas of residence. It is characteristic of an urbanised and highly differentiated society that the normal person belongs to several different 'places' at the same time — the place of his residence, the place of his work, and perhaps the place of his other cultural interests. In this sense one has to say that everyone belongs at the same time to several neighbourhoods. The 'neighbour' is not just the one so defined by geographical propinquity of residence. There is therefore need that the forms of the church should include congregations which are based on these other neighbourhoods. I do not think that the geographical parish can ever become irrelevant or marginal. There is a sense in which the primary sense of neighbourhood must remain primary, because it is here that men and women relate to each other simply as human beings and not in respect of their functions in society. But it is clear,

I think, that alongside these geographically defined units of the Church's corporate life, there is need for other basic Christian congregations shaped by the other kinds of neighbourhood. The corollary of this will be that it is essential for the Church also to have strongly developed units of a larger kind in which these smaller units can join from time to time in forms of celebration, worship and fellowship which transcend these narrower divisions.

What is also clear is that the development of these more flexible patterns of congregational life will call for much more flexible and varied styles of ministry. The assumption that the ministry must normally be a full-time salaried profession is a survival from the Constantinian settlement which cannot rule our present thinking. It is an obviously and often-noted fact that the most rapidly growing churches in the world today are — in general — those which make full use of a non-stipendiary ministry developed by the methods of apprenticeship from within the membership of the whole church. My own experience as a missionary in India has convinced me that the rapid expansion of the Church into unevangelised areas can best be achieved by analogous methods — trusting the Holy Spirit both to find His own way of bringing men and women to Christian faith and to equip those so converted with the gifts needed to lead others into that faith. I have seen the Church grow through the multiplication of new congregations which were led from the beginning by the new converts themselves. Here the traditionally trained and salaried ministers of the Church served to encourage, support and train the local leaders — who were ordinary farmers, shopkeepers or labourers. The leadership remained in the hands of these local people and the Churches grew and multiplied by a process of spontaneous communication along the natural lines of human relationships. On the other hand I have seen (very frequently, it must be said) the opposite process at work. Here the local man or woman whose spiritual experience has been the starting point of the movement towards the Gospel is quietly elbowed aside and the salaried professional takes charge. The movement of spontaneous growth withers and dies; in its place there is a laborious and — in fact — endless struggle to lift the new congregation to the level of attainment which has been fixed by the seminary or college in which the salaried worker was trained. The village congregation remains dependent upon a leadership which is trained, directed and supported from outside. It ceases to be a centre of spontaneous growth.

I am sure that these Indian experiences are not irrelevant to the situation in western industrialised society. I have met, for example, men working on the shop-floor in a big factory, including people holding positions of leadership as shop stewards, who have come to a fresh experience of Christ and who are eager to share their faith. The question which immediately arises is whether they can develop into a living Christian community with their own leadership conforming to the language, style and culture of their community, or whether they have to emigrate from their culture, attach themselves to one of the middle-class congregations in the neighbourhood, and depend permanently for leadership upon men trained in the style of a typical English college or seminary. I do not see any possibility for the spontaneous communication of the

Gospel and the growth of a living Christian community in this working-class milieu unless something like the Indian example which I have quoted is followed. This would mean that men and women who belong to the culture of industrial labour and earn their living on the shop-floor should at the same time be ordained to the full ministry of word and sacrament so that they can become the leaders of Christian congregations which are truly part of that culture.

I know from experience that this proposal meets with strong resistance from those who cannot conceive of the ministry in other terms than those which have been bequeathed to us by the 'Christendom' experience. But modern industrial society is a highly complex organism of differentiated but overlapping communities in each of which men and women have to live their working lives, interact with others and take daily and hourly decisions on highly complex and difficult issues. The ministerial leadership of the Church in such communities must be part of their life, understanding its pressures and its complexities and its ethical ambiguities. Only with such leadership can there develop in each of these communities — be it factory, university, city council, professional association or whatever — living Christian cells which can function as a sign and foretaste of God's reign for those communities. Only in this way can we expect to see visible expressions of the life of the Church where the powers of evil are recognised, unmasked and challenged, where the sin of the world is borne, where the power of the resurrection is made credible, where a sign of the kingdom is erected.

4. One final point must be made, and it is this. The more we stress the need that the Church should develop a new open-ness to the world, a new flexibility in its structures and new styles of ministerial leadership to meet the changing patterns of secular life, the more necessary it is to stress the centrality and finality of Jesus Christ for everything in the life of the Church, the fundamental reality of personal conversion to him and of confession of his name. With the kind of openness and flexibility which I have advocated, it may be difficult to say exactly where the boundaries of the Church lie; this does not matter provided we are clear and make clear to others where the centre lies. An entity can be defined either in terms of its boundaries or in terms of its centre. The Church is an entity which is properly described by its centre. It is impossible to define exactly the boundaries of the Church, and the attempt to do so always ends in an unevangelical legalism. But it is always possible and necessary to define the centre. The Church is its proper self, and is a sign of the Kingdom, only insofar as it continually points men and women beyond itself to Jesus and invites them to personal conversion and commitment to him.

I have drawn attention to what happens when abstract nouns such as 'justice' and 'liberation' are substituted for the active verbs which are the typical form of the biblical language — verbs which have as their ever-present subject the living God who liberates, who forgives, who heals. There is a profound difference between commitment to a cause which can use these great words as its slogans, and commitment to the person who is the subject of these verbs. Personal commitment to Jesus Christ, continually renewed through a continually repeated re-incorporation into his dying and his resurrection, is something which can never be equated with commitment to a cause. The essential character of Christian action for justice, liberation and healing will be that it is simply an outflowing of a new reality — namely the life of the crucified and risen Lord in whom we already become sharers in the new creation. When we separate the cause from the person, when we separate the kingdom from the king, we fall into ideology and we become the victims of the law instead of bearers of the gospel.

I have used the word 'sign' frequently, trying always to insist that the Church is a sign of the kingdom only insofar as it points men and women to Jesus who is himself the one sign of the kingdom. Jürgen Moltmann in his book 'The Church in the Power of the Spirit' has drawn attention to what happens when the Church is eager to find 'signs of the kingdom' apart from Jesus himself. He draws attention to the way in which the French Revolution was confidently hailed as such a 'sign' — by some who saw in it the dawn of the new age, and by others who saw in it the rising of the Beast out of the Abyss! There are uncomfortable parallels to be found in contemporary Christian writing. Perhaps it is only necessary to say the word 'China' in order to illustrate what I mean!

In the New Testament it is clear that the only sign of the Kingdom is Jesus himself. The central task of the Church, as it prays 'Your Kingdom Come!' is to bear witness to him in whom the kingdom *has* come, to call all men to that U-turn in the mind which we call conversion so that they may acknowledge him as King and join his whole Church in the prayer: 'Come, Lord Jesus!'